PUPPY
TRAINING
101

The Essential Guide to Raising a Puppy With Love.
Train Your Puppy and Raise the Perfect Dog
Through Potty Training, Housebreaking, Crate
Training and Dog Obedience.

CESAR DUNBAR

Medical Disclaimer: This book does not contain any medical advice. The ideas and suggestions contained in this book are not intended as a substitute for consulting with your veterinary doctor. All matters regarding you and your puppy's health require medical supervision.

Legal Disclaimer: all photos used in this book are licensed for commercial use or in the public domain.

ERRORS

Please contact us if you find any errors.

We have taken every effort to ensure the quality and correctness of this book. However, after going over the book draft time and again, we sometimes don't see the forest for the trees anymore.

If you notice any errors, we would really appreciate it if you could contact us directly before taking any other action. This allows us to quickly fix it.

Errors: errors@semsoli.com

REVIEWS

Reviews and feedback help improve this book and the author.

If you enjoy this book, we would greatly appreciate it if you were able to take a few moments to share your opinion and post a review on Amazon.

ENQUIRIES & FEEDBACK

For any general feedback about the book, please feel free to contact us at this email address: **contact@semsoli.com**

Table of Contents

INTRODUCTION

There are very few things in this world that are more exciting than getting a new dog into your life.

Even better if it's a **puppy**!

Aren't puppies just the cutest thing ever?

I don't think there's a living soul in the world who doesn't melt if they hold a puppy in their arms.

Yet they can also be little rascals...

Like children, they need to learn boundaries. They can't help showing puppy behavior. **It's up to you to teach them how to be a dog.**

But your pup is worth it. Dogs give so much in return!

The journey goes way beyond simply having a companion in your life. We have so much to learn from dogs. They:

- live in the moment
- love unconditionally
- never hold any grudges, and
- are never spiteful

All this aside, getting a dog in your home does have its own set of challenges. You will need to teach your new pet a lot of things, so that you and your dog can live in harmony. Training your dog will help in creating a rewarding relationship.

But don't worry: you are in good hands!

This is the *perfect* puppy training guide for you. You will learn all the necessary information you need to turn your puppy into a well-behaving dog!

No fluff.

Each chapter in *Puppy Training 101* is super practical, we're getting straight to the point.

Here are some of the things we are going to cover:

- Getting inside your pup's head: learning to understand his body language
- Crate training, and why should teach it to your pup
- How to teach your pup the 5 most important commands: "Sit", "Stay", "Lie Down", "Recall", and "Heel"
- Housebreaking
- How to correct bad behavior, such as biting, jumping, and excessive barking

- And lots of other tips and strategies that will make all the difference when raising your pup!

A well-trained puppy is a pleasure to have around. Let's learn how to make that happen.

I hope you are excited!

Let's get started, shall we?

CHAPTER 1: GETTING STARTED WITH PUPPY TRAINING

"Training a puppy is like raising a child. Every single interaction is a training opportunity."

Ian Dunbar

Key Takeaway: Puppy training is about getting your puppy to listen to you. It is important to understand what to teach your puppy, when to teach it, and how to teach it.

Puppy training starts as soon as you bring your puppy home. Whatever your pup does, you will need to react in a proper manner, or he will end up learning the wrong things. You must already be anticipating the joys of having a puppy, however it isn't going to be a cakewalk. Puppies are cute little bundles of joy, full of curiosity and a pleasure to be around. However, it can also get exasperating at times. If you are well equipped to respond properly to the challenges of having a new puppy in the house, then the housebreaking period for you and your pup will be shorter and stress free.

There are certain things that you should get right when you are raising a puppy. Routines help in reassuring the puppy. For instance, his bowls for food and water should always be placed in a constant place. You will need to teach your puppy:

- a daily routine
- where his food bowl is placed
- the times of the day when he will get to eat

- where his bed is, the time he needs to go to bed
- the time when he gets up
- when he goes for bathroom, and also
- when he gets to go for a walk or play

It would be a mistake to think that the manner in which these routines are taught wouldn't matter. It does matter. If you make use of the right method of teaching, then your puppy would be a well behaved on and will be happy too. If you make use of the wrong methods to teach, then your puppy will start making his own decisions and try to fit you into his life. It should be the other way around.

Teach With Words

You should teach your puppy a few words after your pup has learned the two most important words. These two words are:

- 'NO', and
- 'GOOD'

It's not just the routines that you will need to teach your pup. You will need to teach it words as well. Whenever your puppy does something that you appreciate, show your appreciation by saying "good", and if your puppy does something undesirable then say "no". You can start with this when your pup is about two months old. These words should be taught in a proper manner. Your body language and tone make all the difference. If you get your puppy when it is more than three months old, you should start teaching these two words immediately.

Biscuit Training Should Be Avoided

Puppies love treats. However, coaxing good behavior with treats should be avoided. Don't rely on treats for training your puppy. You might be wondering what is wrong with it. When you start practicing "biscuit training", you are giving up the decision-making power to your puppy. Depending on whether or not your puppy is hungry, your puppy will decide to listen to you. This allows your puppy to believe that he doesn't have to listen to you.

This doesn't mean that you should deprive your puppy of treats altogether. Treats can be used for motivation, especially while teaching tricks. However, this should be a reward and not the method of teaching itself. Coaxing a puppy to do what you want on a daily basis will not help in training him.

Respect Training

Your puppy will pay attention to you only if he respects you. Your puppy should know that you are the leader at home. Without any respect, your puppy might learn the words and the routines, but will not listen to you. Your puppy's disrespect can be traced back to improper training. Too much of coddling will also lead to it. Your puppy should be taught who's the boss at home, if you want him to listen to you. Respect isn't something that you can get almost right. There needs to be consistency and you should keep doing it regularly.

This book, *Puppy Training 101*, will help you in figuring things out in this respect. A dog can learn a lot of words, and there isn't a better way to get him to understand what you want him to do and not to do, than to choose deliberately the words that you want him to learn. Knowing the words, you want to teach will be of no help, if you don't know how to teach. You don't have to expect your dog to listen to your child's stories. However, you can expect him to listen carefully to you. He should be eager to follow the directions you give him.

Let's take a look at the puppy-training schedule.

Crate Training

You can start crate training when your puppy is two to three months old. A crate will help in protecting your puppy from household accidents and it comes in handy when you want to housebreak your puppy. The crate would be your pup's sanctuary. Don't think of this as a pup's jail. If you do, then your puppy will start thinking the same too.

Initially, your puppy might not be happy to have his movements restricted. But it won't take long before he will go on his own to his crate for catching a quick nap, or to just retreat from all the household activity. For a new puppy, a crate will not only help in housebreaking, but it will also double up as a place for him to sleep in. When your puppy gets used to the crate, it gets really easy to take him to the vet or even for trips in your car.

Housebreaking

When your puppy is two to three months old, you can start with housebreaking training. A two-month old puppy is as good as an infant baby. They won't have much control over their bladder. Especially a small breed puppy. They don't develop control over their bladder for several months. Still, you should start your efforts at housebreaking since you get your puppy home.

Start out by establishing a pattern. This will help your puppy to cooperate with you as well. However, if you get this wrong, housebreaking will be nothing short of a nightmare. Most owners don't realize it until their puppy has had an accident in the house. These accidents will start becoming a routine, and it is really difficult to change this pattern. There are different ways in which you can start this out. This would include making use of a crate, a doggy door, or even a litter box for smaller breeds. You will learn more about this in Chapter 7 – Housebreaking

Acceptance

You will also need to start handling your puppy. This is the only way in which he would accept everything that you do with him. Your puppy will need to see you as the leader in the home. Being the leader doesn't mean that you will simply have to keep deciding what's okay and isn't okay for your puppy.

For instance, brushing, bathing, clipping your pup's nails, putting a collar on, a harness, or even giving your pup a pill. When it comes to these things, it is you and not your puppy that gets to decide what needs to be done. The best way, in which you can do this, would be to include some respect lessons along with the vocabulary lessons. If you teach the words and the puppy respects you too, then acceptance will follow suit.

Gentleness

Furthermore, you will need to teach your puppy that he needs to be gentle while interacting with others. He shouldn't nip or chew on people's hands or feet. Just like with acceptance training, being gentle should also be taught to your dog. A puppy is usually taught gentleness by his mother, when she (firmly) corrects the puppy while playing. Your job is to take over from there. You are your puppy's parent.

So, it is not just about caring, but also about correcting the puppy when he starts going wrong somewhere. You will need to teach your puppy to show restraint. You are the one who gets to set limits about good and bad behavior. Remember this.

Household Rules

You will need to teach your puppy about the behaviors that are acceptable and aren't acceptable in the house. Is he allowed to chew on shoes? No. Is he allowed to jump on someone's lap or sit on the furniture when others are present? You get to decide this, and everyone in the household should follow the same too. Is he allowed to enter the kitchen while food is being cooked? This might be unsafe for the puppy, so probably no. Even simple things like whether or not he is allowed to take socks from the laundry pile, sleeping in your bed at night, or even barking at strangers when he sees them from the window.

You will need to decide on the household rules, and then be consistent in making your puppy listen to you. If you have decided that something isn't acceptable, then convey the same to the others in the house too. You shouldn't confuse your puppy.

Tips for Older Puppies

You might think that the training schedule might be different for an older puppy. Well, it really isn't. Regardless of the age of the puppy, the training schedule should be the same. You will need to start out with vocabulary training. Start out with the basic routine, praise, corrective words, crate training, acceptance training, gentleness, and even household rules. So, if your puppy is still eating off your hand, barking at strangers, or doesn't stop when you tell him to, this would be the right time to start out with the basic training.

Start out with simple and essential words like no and good, before moving onto the words like stay, sit, or even heel. Respect will always need to come first regardless of his age.

Move on to other words after he gets to understand the basic ones. Like walking on the leash without tugging at it, coming to you when called, lying down or staying still, waiting at the door even when it's open, to stop barking when you tell him to and so much more.

All these skills would involve your puppy learning up new words. It is not just about learning what these words mean; it is also about doing what they mean. You will need to teach these words in a specific manner. This will help in your puppy seeing you as a leader. Giving him treats won't be of any help.

Leadership definitely doesn't mean hitting your puppy, or making use of choke collars. There are certain little things that you will need to do and say while interacting with your puppy. All puppies will misbehave from time to time. However, the manner in which you respond to them makes all the difference.

If you keep responding in the wrong manner, then the puppy will keep on misbehaving. If you respond in a desirable manner, he will think of you as the leader. It is best if you can get this right since the beginning. With a new puppy, you get the chance to teach him all the right habits and correct them whenever he does something wrong.

CHAPTER 2: HOW DOES A PUPPY THINK?

"There is no psychiatrist in the world like a puppy licking your face."

Bernard Williams

Key Takeaways: Take a psychological peek into your puppy's dreams, emotions, interests, tail wagging, and body language.

Ever wondered what your dog is thinking about? Read on to find out more. Would you like to know what your dog might be thinking? Wouldn't that be wonderful? Perhaps you have thought of a situation where your dog is able to clearly communicate with you. Unfortunately, this is nothing more than wishful thinking. However, you can develop a basic understanding of the psychology of your puppy.

Staring

"What are you thinking?" you might wonder, as your puppy is looking at you longingly. If you have already fed him and have also taken him out for a walk, it might be really difficult to figure out what he is thinking. Dogs tend to gaze at their owners, intently. Probably this isn't a sign of boredom. He is probably staring at you intently because he wants a treat, wants to play, or just wants you to pet him for a while. Your dog might also be doing this because he wants some extra attention and love.

Looking Sad

Do you feel really guilty when you leave your puppy home alone and head out to work the whole day? You might worry that your dog would be sad the whole day. Unless your puppy has separation anxiety, your puppy will be perfectly fine. In fact, if you have a dog walker checking in on your dog, then the puppy would greet him with a wagging tail. Your puppy might seem confused or even sad when you leave, but they tend to get used to your routine. They tend to adapt themselves to it. However, it is really important that your dog knows the difference between your usual work schedule and a long trip.

Barking Repeatedly

Does your puppy tend to keep barking whole night long? It might seem like the only reason he's doing this is to keep you from getting any sleep. You will need to remember that they bark for a particular reason. Your puppy isn't barking to annoy you. Your puppy might be doing this to get your attention.

A dog usually barks when it wants something. Perhaps a treat, to go on a walk, or even to be freed from its confinement. It could also be because your puppy senses danger and he wants to let you know. Or he is excited and wants to play with you. Dogs tend to learn by repeating their behaviors. If your puppy has discovered that by barking, he gets something that he wants, he will keep on doing it.

Cocking Their Head

You might have noticed that your dog tends to tilt his head to the side when you speak to him. This is definitely not because your puppy understands the story you are telling him. They tend to cock their head for multiple reasons. Your puppy might be hoping to better understand a word you are saying, or something that sounds familiar. Your puppy might also be cocking his head so that he can hear you better. Or perhaps to get a better look at your face to understand what you are saying.

Attempting to understand what goes on within your puppy's mind is an ongoing practice. After a while, you will be able to understand what your dog wants by just one look of theirs.

CHAPTER 3: BENEFITS OF CRATE TRAINING

""I'll put her in charge of the puppies. I've twelve this week that need tending. How does that suit you?" Leeli's mouth hung open. She tried to say something but instead crumpled to the floor. She had fainted with joy."

Andrew Peterson – The Monster in the Hollows

Key Takeaway: A crate helps in bringing out the natural denning instinct present in puppies. There are multiple benefits to crate training.

There are many benefits of using a crate. It comes in handy while you are taking your pup to the vet, to a kennel, a hotel, or even while you are travelling by air. Training your puppy to use a crate is helpful. Let us take a look at the benefits that you and your pup can enjoy by making use of a crate.

Helps in Housebreaking

Puppies have an inherent sense of denning, the trait that they have inherited from their ancestors. This means that they would keep their den, the place that they eat and sleep at, clean of urine and feces. This can be made use of for decreasing the time required to housebreak your pup and avoid any little accidents.

When you have placed your pup in the crate, they will definitely refrain from going to the toilet for as long as they possibly can. You can place your pup in the crate for a short period and then immediately take them out to their toilet area.

Encourage them, and they will definitely do the deed. Therefore, instead of roaming around the house and soiling wherever they wish to, they would wait for you to take them outside.

Hinders Destructive Chewing

Most of the puppies and adult dogs tend to chew a lot, especially while they are teething. If you want to save your household items, then it is important that you teach them what they should and shouldn't chew. If your pup regularly chews on something, and it is allowed to do so, then this will become a habit. If your pup chews on slippers, cushions, shoes, or anything else regularly, then this will become a habit for him.

If you are supervising your puppy and you see this behavior, then you can redirect your pup to chew something more acceptable. However, if supervision isn't possible, then you can place them in the crate with their chew toys. This will teach your pup to chew on the correct toys and prevent them from chewing the wrong ones.

It Keeps Your Dog Safe

If you aren't able to supervise your puppy constantly and there are a lot of opportunities for them to get into any form of trouble, then keep them in their crate. Trouble could mean causing damage to your belongings, or putting themselves in dangerous situations.

Prevents the Formation of Problem Behaviors

Dogs like to seek rewards. They will behave in different ways till they find the one that will help them seek a reward. The pup will repeat the same habit in the future for getting the reward. This is how their habits are formed. Digging in the yard or eating the contents of the fridge could be rewarding for the dog, but undesirable for you. If you happen to catch them, then you can correct their behavior. However, what to do when you aren't around? Crating your pup when you can't be around so that they will not engage in any unwanted behaviors will prevent the formation of bad habits. As they start growing older, the time that they spend in the crate will also keep decreasing.

Safety and Security

A crate would be your pup's special place. A crate would be their own place, it will provide them some peace, quiet, and refuge for them to relax and sleep. A crate is like its own den. How a child would feel in their own room, a dog would feel the same in its crate.

For Solving Behavioral Problems

Training and management will help in solving your pup's behavioral problems. You will need to train your pup to stop engaging in any undesirable behavior and teach them good behavior. Management would be to prevent your pup from having an opportunity to perform any bad behavior. This combination will help in preventing your dog from engaging in any undesirable behavior and enforcing desirable behavior. You can crate your puppy when you aren't able to prevent them from engaging in any undesirable behavior.

Calming Your Puppy

The best tool for a time out would be a crate. If you want to take your puppy out of an environment for calming them from their overexcited state, then the crate is the best option. They can get overexcited when playing with another dog or even while playing any vigorous game with you.

Safe Travel

For air travel, your puppy will need to be crated. If they are used to being in a crate anyway, then they will be calmer and ready for the whole experience. They don't need to be crated while in a car, but it will be better if they are. An unrestrained dog might suffer injuries in the case of an accident in a car. He also might be a distraction for the driver and climb out of the window.

CHAPTER 4: CRATE TRAINING 101

"As to which is cuter, a puppy or a baby, I'm going to say that probably depends less on the particular puppy and more on the baby. I've seen pictures of me as an infant and consider myself lucky that nobody ever offered my parents the opportunity to trade me for a beagle."

W. Bruce Cameron

Key Takeaway: When the puppy is crate trained, the puppy can be made to travel safely and without any hassles. The puppy would have his own space to retreat to; it helps in housebreaking too. Crate training doesn't take long.

In the previous chapter, we learned about the different benefits of crate training. In this chapter, let us get started with the basics of crate training.

Introducing The Crate

It is very likely that your puppy hasn't spent much time in a crate before, except when he had to travel or when the breeder has started him with housebreaking.

Therefore, crate training will be new to your pup. The one reason why it is effective is because of your puppy's instinct to keep his den clean. In the wild, the puppies would go out of their den for eliminating. Even if it meant to just take two steps into the wild. This instinct is hardwired into their brains. Your puppy has never probably seen a real den.

Being in a crate will trigger their instinctive behavior and he will try his best to not soil his crate. Crate training a puppy definitely helps in making housebreaking easier. A puppy would always want to be next to his pack. Well, you are his pack now. He would feel anxious if he were away from you. This might be the reason why your puppy will cry, whine, or even make a fuss about being in his crate. He doesn't hate the crate, he just feels vulnerable when you aren't around. Your puppy is safe in there, however your puppy doesn't know that yet. He's a domesticated dog, so it will take a while for your puppy to get used to being away from you.

You should just let your pup get used to the crate, this will make him feel comfortable around it before he can spend time inside it. While crate training, you shouldn't ever make use of the crate as a form of punishment. The crate needs to be his safe den. It needs to be his refuge. He won't have a positive attitude towards it if you make use of it as a punishment. It needs to be your puppy's happy place. Here are a few rules and ideas that will help your puppy get used to his new crate.

There needs to be open access. Initially, you should leave the door to the crate open and place a few treats inside the crate. A puppy's curiosity will make him venture inside the crate and enjoy his treats.

Furthermore, you can also feed your puppy in the crate. This will help the puppy in forming an association between meals and his crate. The puppy might seem a little hesitant to feed inside the crate but will get used to it.

You can also make crate training seem fun to your puppy by playing hide and seek. You will need to place a toy or a treat inside the crate and ask your puppy to find it. You can say something encouraging like "where's your treat? Let us go find it!" You will need to follow this up by praising him when he finds it. You can say something like "oh there it is! Inside your crate! Good boy!"

Crate Training Safety

A crate will help in keeping your puppy safe. However, here are a few things that you can do for making sure that he stays safe in there. Don't ever chain your puppy while placing him in the crate. Avoid slip collars as well. These things tend to get caught up in things. This will cause him to panic and it could be quite tragic. Make sure that the collar is an undecorated collar.

When the puppy is in the crate, make sure that there is sufficient ventilation in the room or wherever he is placed. Don't ever leave the puppy in the crate in a room that is hot, don't place it under direct sunlight or leave it in a car on a hot day.

While you are crate training your puppy, make sure that children don't tease him. Don't let them push their fingers into the crate through the wire or tease your puppy. This will make your puppy feel threatened, which can lead him to get aggressive for no fault of his own.

CHAPTER 5: HOW TO TEACH YOUR PUPPY ROUTINES

"Whenever I want to laugh, I read a wonderful book, 'Children's Letters to God.' You can open it anywhere. One I read recently said, 'Dear God, thank you for the baby brother, but what I prayed for was a puppy'."

Maya Angelou

Key Takeaway: A routine helps in creating familiarity for your puppy. Familiarity helps in making your puppy feel safe and secure. Also, the puppy will know what is expected of it and when.

Puppies are definitely merry little creatures. However, while training a puppy it really does help to have a routine in place for making your puppy feel secure. Creating a routine for your puppy will not only let your puppy know the rules. It will also help him understand what you want and don't want him to do. Remember that when you are getting a puppy home, it is a big change for the puppy as well.

You are taking the puppy away from everything that is familiar to him and placing him in an environment that is very strange to him. Even the most confident of pups would get scared. Having a schedule helps in providing some form of familiarity to the puppy. It also helps in minimizing any surprises and thereby reduces any stress the pup might feel.

House Rules

Before you take a puppy home, make sure that everyone in the household agrees to certain rules. The puppy will only get confused if there is no consistency. If one person lets the puppy jump onto the sofa and if the other gets angry at the puppy for doing the same, this will just confuse him. For learning, puppies will need consistency. Changing the rules constantly will just confuse your pup and interfere with his ability to learn. Decide beforehand if the puppy should be allowed onto the furniture and the place where he gets to sleep. Whether or not he would have a crate, you get to decide the basic rules. Once you have decided these rules, make sure that everyone in the household agrees to these.

Potty Routine

It will be easier for the puppy to know what's expected of him when there's a familiar routine. You should select a location that is not only easy accessible, but can be cleaned easily as well for potty training.

Make sure that everyone in the household is aware of where the puppy needs to "go". Pets tend to get confused if you shift their bathroom. If you stick to one particular area, then the smell and the location will let the puppy know what's expected.

You will need to schedule proper potty breaks for your puppy. It is ideally the first thing in the morning, once after lunch, once in the evening and right before going to bed at night. The number of breaks that your puppy will need to go to will reduce with age. As the puppy matures, the puppy will gain control over his bladder. However, in the beginning make sure that you are sticking to a schedule if you want to avoid any "accidents" in the house. Take him out for a walk as much as possible, especially after every meal when he is not trained yet.

Meal Schedule

You will need to make a schedule for your puppy's meals and also decide on a location. You should decide whether or not the puppy would be allowed to get any treats from the table. Everyone in the household should agree about these things.

You wouldn't want to decide on something only to later on notice that children have been sneaking in food to the puppy. Getting your puppy any treats from the table would not only spoil your puppy's training, but it is bad for the puppy as well. It would also lead to begging as well as stealing food from the table!

Make sure that no one is teasing the puppy with food. Children tend to do this and they shouldn't. It wouldn't be fair to the puppy if you keep insisting that he should eat from his bowl while others sneak him food. Maybe you can come to a compromise. Family members can probably decide to give a few scraps to the puppy, then in such a case, they should place them in his bowl after he finishes his regular meal. You can also make use of these for his training sessions.

Exercise Routine

A puppy that's tired is extremely well behaved. Depending on your puppy's stamina and the way he plays, you can schedule his playtimes. Exercise will not only keep your puppy healthy, but it will also help in wearing him out. When puppies play, it also helps them in bonding with you. Make use of this playtime for teaching some basic obedience commands. Take five minutes every day and have a quick recap of all the lessons that the puppy already knows. You can also teach him some new ones.

CHAPTER 6: THE 5 COMMANDS YOU NEED TO TEACH YOUR PUPPY

"Disaster, to me, means in some big or small way, things going wrong. And that's obviously a matter of perception, right? Let's say your puppy chewed up all the shoes in your house. She probably had a fine time doing that. In her mind, a red letter day, the highlight of her puppy life."

Amy Gerstler

Key Takeaway: Commands can be made use of for making your puppy understand what you want him to do or not to do. You can communicate with your puppy through commands.

In this chapter let us take a look at five basic commands that you will need to teach your puppy. These commands are to make your dog to:

- Sit
- Stay
- Lie Down
- Recall, and
- Heel

These are the five most important commands. They will help you in communicating your wishes to your puppy. Once you are done with these basic commands you can start teaching him more advanced ones.

Teaching Your Puppy to Sit

You will have to start out by teaching your puppy how to sit when given the command to do so. Your puppy shows politeness by sitting. This is a natural form of reaction and shows that the dog isn't aggressive. It also shows the puppy's willingness to wait.

When you enforce this command, the puppy will learn that if he wants something, or if you are busy, then the proper thing to do would be to sit and wait. The aim of teaching your puppy this command is that it would tell him when he is supposed to sit and pay attention or to just calm down.

You will need to stand right in front of your puppy. Be calm but assertive. For getting your puppy's attention, you will need to look him in the eye and say "[*your dog's name*], sit."

Initially, you can hold up a treat just above your puppy's nose. In order for your puppy to see the treat, your puppy will need to keep its head up and in this process his bum will go down.

As soon as your puppy sits, give some praise. You can say "Yes" or "Good Boy" and then give the treat that he was promised. The goal is for your puppy to associate the action or the word with the treat and the praise that he would get for doing it.

As much as possible, make use of hand signals instead of offering treats. Once your dog gets accustomed to the verbal command, then you can use a hand signal to convey the same. The most common one would be by placing the flat of your hand over your dog's ahead and in front of it while you say, "Sit". You will have to keep repeating this over and over again till your dog gets a hang of it. You will need to be patient and keep trying. It is really important that your dog follows your lead and not the other way around.

Teaching the Command "Stay"

There are certain commands that can help in saving your dog's life and "Stay" happens to be one of those commands. This command will help in avoiding any dangerous situations and also with keeping your dog out of trouble. A pup will understand the command stay easily since it is instinctive for it.

You will have to start out by training your dog to assume the "sit" position. When your dog sits, you will have to stand facing the same direction as your dog. This will be referred to as the "place" stance or position.

Now, you will have to hold the collar of your dog and say its name, followed by the command "Stay". Do this by placing your palm in front of the dog's face. However, it shouldn't touch your dog. Your fingertips should be pointing upwards and your palm should be towards your dog. If your dog stays still, then reward it with a treat and some praise. If your dog gets up, then start all over again. Keep repeating till your dog understands what it is supposed to do.

Once your dog understands this command, then you can proceed towards increasing the amount of time spent following this command. Gradually increase the amount of time for which your dog should stay still. If your dog tends to get up somewhere in between, then you will have to start all over again. You will also need to keep moving around while your dog is staying still. There needs to be a release word that you can make use of for letting your dog know that it can move now. You can use words like "okay or come".

To Lay Down

You will need to teach your dog to lie down. This command is usually combined with the "Stay" command, but is a relatively stronger command. "Down" should be made use of for stopping whatever action was taking place before the command was given. It helps in controlling or restraining the dog's behavior.

You will have to start out with the "Sit" and then say your dog's name followed by "Down". You should hold your left hand over your dog's head and the palm should be pointing towards the floor. Hold a treat in your right hand. Lower the hand towards the floor slowly and keep it close to your dog's body. You will need to keep giving your dog some form of positive reinforcement for completing this command.

Once your dog has placed itself on the floor with its elbows and bum resting on the floor, you can give it some praise. This will help in forming a positive association between the action performed and the reward it gets. You will need to keep repeating this command several times till your dog actually gets a hang of it.

The goal is for your dog or your puppy to learn and follow the command. The dog will need to follow the command regardless of what it is. In this manner, you will be able to stop your dog before it indulges in any destructive behavior. Like with any other commands, you will have to start from the beginning if your dog doesn't listen to you.

Teaching Recall

You will need to teach your dog to come to you whenever you call him. Recall is also referred to as "come". You will have to start out with the basic "sit" position and then move ahead from there.

Start by gently pulling your dog by its collar while saying its name, followed by "Come". You should do this in an encouraging voice. You want your dog to come to you and this should be accompanied with a gesture of your hand to show the dog what you want it to do. You can lure your dog towards you with the help of a treat or even by placing a bit of dog food at your feet and point at it.

After gesturing for a while, your dog will definitely come towards the food. It is incredibly important that you keep on providing your dog with some form of positive reinforcement so that he knows that he is doing the right thing. Positive encouragement and treats will definitely help the dog know that what he is doing is desirable.

You will need to keep practicing this command time and again. Whenever you are interacting with your pet, and at any opportunity you get practice this command. If your dog does something else instead of coming towards you, you will have to start all over again.

Teaching Your Dog to Heel

This is perhaps one of the most difficult commands to teach your dog. However, with time and consistency, your dog will definitely learn it. Teaching your puppy to heel will not only save your back, shoulders and neck, but will also help in saving your dog's neck. Not just that, it will also help in saving your dignity and your dog's too.

However, dignity might not be something that your dog would care much for. Your dog would probably want to walk at a brisk pace, sniff, and keep veering off in different directions. You will need to tell him whether or not it is the time for him to go exploring.

Start out by placing your dog in the sitting position. Make use of the usual leash with which you take him for walking with and get your dog to "sit" beside your leg. You both should be facing the same direction. This is referred to as the place position. Make use of the left side to not confuse your dog.

Now say your dog's name and say "heel". Say this while you are stepping forward with the left food. This will tell your dog that it is time to move forward. Your dog will either try to resist or zoom ahead. In such a case, gently tug on his leash and repeat this command again. You will need to keep instructing your dog to stay by your side. You can pat your leg and say, "Keep with me or over here". Make sure you say this affirmatively. Your dog should want to follow your command.

If your dog starts moving ahead of you, you should say your dog's name and say heel in a very calm and authoritative voice. If necessary, tug on his leash and ask him to sit down. If your dog resists or moves ahead, then pull him gently and place him near your left leg. There shouldn't be any tension between you and your dog. Your dog should want to listen to you. Keep your calm and stay patient.

This command does take a while to get right. Don't forget to give your dog some praise whenever he gets it right. You will also have to teach your dog to stop and sit whenever you stop. When you think you are ready to stop, stop yourself on your left foot and calmly say, "sit". After repeating this for a few times, your dog will definitely get the hang of it.

Practice this command with just your body language. After a while, your dog will understand what you mean. You can make use of hand signals or verbal commands, whatever works the best.

There are certain things that you should keep in mind while training your dog.

You should never show your frustration or any irritation you might feel while training. This will just confuse your dog or even frighten it. This will create a negative experience not just for your dog but for you as well. If you feel that you are losing your calm, then in such a case, take a break and start again. Stay positive. Your dog should feel rewarded too.

You should be firm and gentle with your dog. Don't let him take advantage of you. You shouldn't postpone the training sessions or give up too quickly. It is easier to start training a pup than a dog, the choice is yours.

Make sure that the dog knows who the boss is before you get started with the training sessions. The dog won't listen to you if it doesn't think that you are the leader.

Finally, don't involve too many peoples when it comes to training your dog. If the dog hears different things at one go, it will just get confused.

CHAPTER 7: HOUSEBREAKING YOUR PUPPY IN 4 EASY STEPS

"I'm not alone," said the boy. "I've got a puppy."

Jane Thayer – The Puppy Who Wanted a Boy

Key Takeaway: Housebreaking your puppy helps in establishing a happy and conflict free relationship. Only when the puppy is housebroken can you let the puppy walk around freely.

Consistency, patience, and lots of positive reinforcement are required for housetraining your puppy. The goal of this exercise is to help in building certain good habits in your puppy and to establish a loving bond with it. It can take anywhere between four to six months for your puppy to be house trained. However, for some puppies it could take up to a year as well. Size could be major factor too.

A smaller puppy has a smaller bladder and a higher rate of metabolism than a bigger pup. Therefore, a smaller puppy would need to be taken out more frequently. The living conditions of the pup should also be taken into consideration. Furthermore, you might have to get rid of any undesirable habits of your puppy and establish desirable ones. You will need to set a schedule and stick to it.

Have Patience

You will also need to show consistency and patience. Remember that you are dealing with a puppy; a puppy doesn't understand our language. A puppy simply picks on your tone and nonverbal cues. When you are training your puppy, you will definitely face some setbacks. These setbacks aren't a reason for you to give up on training the puppy. As long as you keep on managing them, your puppy will be fine. You should take your puppy out as soon as you see signs that he might want to eliminate and offer him rewards when he does potty outside. This will help him learn.

When to Start Housetraining

Housetraining can be started when the pup is 12 to 16 weeks old. At this age, the pup can control his bladder and bowel movements. Any later than this, it will take longer for you to housetrain your puppy. If your puppy has been used to eliminating in his cage, then it will definitely take you longer for breaking this routine and incorporating a desirable habit instead. Encouragement and reward will help in housetraining your puppy.

It is believed that confining the space that is available to your puppy helps in housetraining. The puppy will not eliminate where it sleeps or eats food. Therefore, it would want to go outside to do his business. Here are some steps that you can follow for housetraining your puppy.

Create a Schedule

You will need to establish a schedule for your puppy and feed it according to this schedule. Don't leave any food in the pup's bowl in between meals. Take the puppy for a walk as soon as he wakes up in the morning, after his meal, after he wakes up from a nap, and even after playing. Take him out to pee after every one hour or so.

Also, make sure that you take him out before he goes to sleep. Take your puppy to the same spot every time so that he can do his business. The smell will also prompt him to do so. You will also need to stay outside with him till he is housetrained. Whenever your puppy has done his business, you should praise him or even give him a treat. A walk can be a treat as well.

Using a Crate

You can make use of a crate as well. However, don't keep your puppy in the crate for more than two hours at a time. Only let him sleep in the crate during the night. The crate should be of a comfortable size. If it is too big then the pup could use this as a bathroom. If it were too small then it wouldn't be comfortable for him. If you can't be with your puppy all through the training period, then you will need to get someone to take care of the puppy and take him for a walk when you aren't at home. You should stop using the crate if you notice that your puppy is using it for eliminating.

Sniffing the ground, barking, whining, circling a spot, or scratching the door are the common signs that your puppy needs to go out. Accidents are bound to happen during potty training. You will need to deal with these incidents properly.

Don't be harsh with your puppy or shout at it. Instead, clean the area thoroughly and take the puppy outside. If you can monitor the puppy, then saying no the moment you see it get ready to eliminate will help too.

CHAPTER 8: HOW TO CORRECT BAD BEHAVIOR

"Puppies are constantly inventing new ways to be bad. It's fascinating. You come into a room they've been in and see pieces of debris and try to figure out what you had that was made from wicker or what had been stuffed with fluff."

Julie Klam – You Had Me at Woof: How Dogs Taught Me the Secrets of Happiness

Key Takeaway: It is essential to correct any bad behavior exhibited by the puppy. Puppies are full of energy and always excited. It is essential to teach them what is right and what is wrong.

You've got a cute, cuddly puppy home and then, the puppy turns out to be a little menace and is creating as much trouble as possible. Your puppy will need to be taught what it can and cannot do. Before you get started with correcting the bad behavior, it will help if you have already taught your dog certain basic commands like sit, stay, come, and down.

Dogs Need Rules

There needs to be consistency in your dog's life. There need to be a few ground rules too. All the family members should use the same method for training or disciplining the puppy. A dog, regardless of its age, will do as it pleases if not trained. You will always need to stay calm and composed whenever you are correcting your dog's behavior. You shouldn't yell, scream, shout, or hit the dog. You don't want your dog to fear you.

Training Your Puppy

Basic obedience training can help in correcting any form of bad behavior. Your pet should be trained so that he understands the basic verbal or hand commands. This should be done when your puppy is about three or four months old. In basic training, all the commands that you have read about in the earlier chapters should be included.

When your puppy is about 10 weeks old, you can train it to sit. There are obedience trainers as well who can help train a puppy as young as 10 weeks. An added benefit is that these classes will help your puppy to socialize with other dogs as well.

Common dog behavior problems are:

- biting / chewing
- jumping onto people
- playing rough
- begging
- excessive barking, and
- digging

Let's take a look at each of them.

Stop Your Dog From Biting and Chewing

It is very natural for the puppy to make use of his mouth when he is playing. He probably did this with his litter pals, and it is also a dog's way of asking the other dog or person to back off. Puppies tend to have really sharp teeth. Whenever you are playing with your puppy, you will definitely want to discourage biting or mouthing in any form.

The way in which you can do this is by letting out a little cry and saying something like "ouch". This will startle the puppy and desist what he's doing. Praise him whenever he stops and you can give him a chewy or a toy as a replacement. If the puppy does have his teeth in your hand, then just let out a loud cry and don't pull away. This will make him stop biting. Praise him immediately when he does so. This will let him know that you are happy that he let go of your hand.

You will have to correct any inappropriate chewing that your dog engages in. Puppies love to chew, especially while teething. Leather shoes and furniture happen to be soft targets. Invest in good chew toys and edible chewable items.

This will help your puppy to understand what he can and cannot chew on. He will slowly but surely catch on to this and understand what is expected of him.

Stop Jumping

When a dog gets excited, they tend to jump on you. Your dog may get excited when you come home, if visitors come over, or even while taking a walk in the park. There are several different ways in which you can get your dog to stop doing this. The best manner in which you can correct this is by making use of the "Off" command. You can train your dog to do so in a very simple manner.

Get one of your family members or your friends to simply walk in from the door. Your dog should be collared and should be kept on the leash. When there is a knock on the door, make your dog walk till the door and keep a short hold on the leash so that the dog doesn't jump on to them. When he does try to jump, then in such a case, you should tug on his leash and say "off" and then say, "sit".

Once he is sitting and isn't trying to jump, then praise him for being a good boy. The other way would be to simply ignore your dog and not make any eye contact. Do this until your dog settles down, and once he does, you will have to praise him.

Stopping From Playing Rough

When your dog starts playing rough, things can quickly go out of control and the situation can get dangerous. You shouldn't ever encourage your dog to attack you or any body part of yours. This might be adorable when your dog is a puppy, however it could hurt someone else.

Whenever you are playing any game that uses force, like tug of war, then in such a case you should teach your dog "drop it" so that he stops what he's doing. You can say, "drop it" and stop pulling. This should help. If it doesn't, then you can say the command, get up and leave. He will realize that by playing rough, you will not play with him.

Stopping From Begging

Your dog is probably by your side all the time. Especially when you are eating something. The dog would probably just sit and stare at you, begging for food. Most common reason for this is that you have perhaps in the past encouraged this behavior unknowingly. You probably would have given him something that you are eating and he thinks that it is okay for him to beg.

You can stop this behavior by feeding your dog at the same time that you are eating, removing him from the room where you usually eat. You can place him in his crate or keep him outside the house. Whenever he begs, a firm no and asking him to sit and stay will help. Correcting this form of behavior will take some time. So, be patient and persistent while correcting him.

Excessive Barking

You will have to teach your dog a really important command and that's "speak". Get him all worked up by offering a treat and tell him "speak". Whenever he barks, give him a treat for doing so. Once he has got the speak command right, move on to teaching him "quiet". Get him to speak first, and don't give the treat right away this time. Instead hold it in your hand and say "quiet". Whenever, he desists from barking, give him the treat. Therefore, he will associate being quiet with earning a treat.

Dealing With Digging

Digging is an instinctual behavior for dogs. Many tend to dig a spot just to escape from the heat and stay cool. There are different ways in which you can stop this behavior. Vigorous exercise will help in tiring him out and he won't dig. You should confine him to the kennel in the yard or any area that is fenced off so that you can keep an eye on him. As soon as he starts digging, you can reprimand him.

Place chicken wire around the hole(s). The feel of the chicken wire will discourage him from digging and he will stop it. You can also fill up the holes with his own feces and then cover it up with soil. Dogs don't like the smell of their feces. So, this would work. If you happen to have some room in the yard, then you can teach him about the areas where he is allowed to dig. At times, dogs tend to dig holes to just bury their bones. If that's the case then don't allow him to eat his bones in the yard.

Get Some Professional Help

Whenever you have got any problems correcting the behavior of your dog, then there are certain professionals who can help you with your dog. Consult your vet to rule out any health reasons that might be causing your dog's bad behavior. Your vet can also help you in getting in touch with dog trainers.

CHAPTER 9: FINAL TIPS FOR TRAINING YOUR PUPPY

"I love words. Sudoku I don't get into. But crossword puzzles, I just can't - if I get a puppy and I paper train him and I put the - if all of a sudden, I'd open the paper and there's a crossword puzzle - 'No, no, you can't go on that, honey. I'll take it'."

Betty White

Key Takeaway: When your puppy is old enough, you can start training him. Regardless of whether you are training the puppy on your own or taking some professional help, there are certain tips that will help you. Be affectionate, patient, consistent, and listen to your puppy.

In this chapter, let us take a look at some of the tips that you will need to keep in mind while training your puppy.

Listen to Your Puppy

You will need to learn to listen to your puppy. If your puppy seems uncomfortable while meeting another dog, any animal or a human being, don't insist that the puppy has to say hello to them. Your dog is trying to tell you that he is uncomfortable and you will need to respect it. Forcing this issue might create bigger issues down the line.

Lots of Affection

More often than not, people are really good at showing their displeasure to their dog when they get upset. However, they tend to ignore all the good things the dog does. This is a huge mistake. Don't do this. You should give your dog affection, praise, and attention when he does something right. He needs to know that he is a good boy. This is when you should be a little generous with affection you show.

Does the Puppy Really Like It?

Just because the bag of treats says, "dog treats", doesn't mean that your dog will love it automatically. Just like with human beings, dogs are selective about what they eat. So, keep your eye open and figure out the kind of things he likes and genuinely enjoys.

Tell Him What He Should Do

You can make use of the "no" command to tell your dog that he shouldn't do something. However, this doesn't provide your dog with much information. Instead of just telling him no, you should tell him what you want him to do. Dogs aren't good with generalizations. If he greets someone by jumping onto them, then saying no wouldn't be of much help. He might jump a little higher, move to the other side. Instead you should tell him what he is supposed to do after stopping the action he was engaged in. So, instead tell him to sit down. That would provide the puppy with some clarity.

Consistency

There needs to be consistency whenever you are training your dog. It is really important that all the family members are on the same page when it comes to training your puppy. You cannot say that something is not okay while someone else allows the puppy to do that very same behavior. The puppy will get confused.

Also, make sure that you all use the same words to communicate with the puppy. Someone might say "off" to get him off the couch or "down" to do the same. In such a case, the dog gets really confused. You should avoid this.

Realistic Expectations

Changing behavior takes a lot of time. You will need to have certain realistic expectations. It takes a while to change those behaviors that you find undesirable in the dog. Usually, the regular doggie habits are the ones that take a long time to change. These include barking, digging, and jumping to greet. It also depends on the amount of time the dog spent rehearsing such behaviors.

For instance, if your puppy was used to jumping to greet people and you let this go on for a long period of time, then you cannot expect to change such a behavior in a short period of time. It takes a while to undo these behaviors and inculcate new ones.

Good Diet

The diet that you give your dog is of great importance. The diet should depend on the amount of activity he is involved in.

For instance, a dog that is used to herding sheep will need more protein than a dog that's indoors all the time. A high protein diet is usually good. Make sure that your puppy gets used to eating dog food instead of human food. Good diet is essential for the overall wellbeing of your puppy. Check with the vet and then proceed with any diet.

Reinforcement

If your dog is exhibiting behaviors that you don't like, there is a really strong likelihood that it was something that was reinforced before.

For instance, if your dog brings you his toy and barks at you to throw it, you throw the toy. Your dog has now learned that barking will get him what he wants. You say no to stop this and your dog starts barking even more. You might give in and throw it. This just makes your dog believe that persistence is the key. So, instead of giving in, you can tell your dog to do something else. You can probably ask him to sit or stay quiet.

Bribery Doesn't Work

Don't use treat to bribe your dog. A treat should be a reward and it shouldn't be a bribe to get him to do something. When you do this, you end up giving the dog the decision-making power. You should avoid this at any cost. Your dog will get to decide whether or not it wants to do something.

Lessons should be a learning activity for the puppy and not something he gets to choose. Your dog should want to do the things you ask of it, when you want.

Freedom

Your dog should earn its freedom in the house. But make this a gradual process. Most of the pet owners tend to give their pet all the freedom it wants. When you do this, you are giving him too much freedom and giving it too soon. This can not only lead to avoidable housebreaking accidents, but can also instill destructive behavior patterns in the puppy. If there are any unoccupied rooms, make use of a baby gate to seal it off.

The best way in which you can make sure that your dog stays safe is to keep him tethered to you. Start out by showing him those places where he can be safe and you can also keep an eye out on him.

CONCLUSION

Getting a puppy home is one of the most wonderful things ever.

Those 2 staring eyes would warm anyone's heart. Even if they belong to that little pup that just trashed the kitchen...

However, you can have your cake *and* eat it!

With everything you have learned in this book *Puppy Training 101*, you now have all the tools and techniques you need to train your pup and turn him into a well-behaving dog.

Here are some of the things you learned:

- How to teach your pup the 5 most important commands: "Sit", "Stay", "Lie Down", "Recall", and "Heel"
- Understanding your pup's body language
- Crate training
- Housebreaking, and

- How to correct bad behavior, such as biting, jumping, and excessive barking

It will take some time, effort, and patience to train your pup. But trust me, it's so worth it!

Start out with simple word training. Teach your puppy to understand certain basic words and commands. Once this is done, you can start with crate training. Respect training and acceptance training should be started immediately. Housebreaking takes a while, so start as soon as you can. Once you have got these things down, you can start teaching your puppy some tricks. And remember: Don't ever lose your patience with your puppy and keep trying.

Finally, without realizing it, you are also building a *relationship* with your puppy. If you teach him boundaries with love and care, it will not only learn what it can and cannot do, but also that you can be trusted.

And he will pay you back tenfold!

I wish you and your puppy all the best – and lots of fun! – when applying everything you have learned.

Let's end on a light note: What's a dog's favorite kind of pizza?

Pupperoni!

:)

DID YOU LIKE THIS BOOK?

If you enjoyed this book, I would like to ask you for a favor. Would you be kind enough to share your thoughts and post a review of this book on Amazon? Just a few sentences would already be really helpful.

Your voice is important for this book to reach as many people as possible.

The more reviews this book gets, the more dog lovers will be able to find it and learn how to properly train their puppy.

Thank you again for reading this book and good luck with applying everything you have learned!

I'm rooting for you…

NOTES

CPSIA information can be obtained
at www.ICGtesting.com
Printed in the USA
FSOW02n0505290118
43920FS